INCREASE
KIDS

VOLUME ONE

DISCLAIMER

Every effort has been made to recreate events, locales, and
conversations as accurately as possible from the memories of those
sharing their stories. In some instances, names of individuals, places,
identifying characteristics, and details such as physical properties,
occupations, and places of residence have been changed to protect
the privacy of individuals.

CREDITS

EDITORS-IN-CHIEF & CREATIVE DIRECTORS
DAVE & TAFF HARVEY

COPY EDITOR
PAM SPINOSI

CONTRIBUTING EDITORS
NATALIE SHAW
CASSANDRA BECK

DESIGN DIRECTOR
BREE STEVENS

CONTRIBUTING WRITERS
CASSANDRA BECK
PAM SPINOSI
AMY GAGNON
LISA EKSTROM
KAREN CRANFILL
ANDREW PHILLIPS
DAVE HARVEY

MARKETING CONSULTANT
KEWYN APPADOO

VIDEO PRODUCTION
JARED RICHARD

KIDS VIDEO TEAM
AMY GAGNON
LISA EKSTROM

———

Thank you to the leadership team of Bethel Christian School and Bethel Healing Rooms for modeling the power of the testimony.

"EVERY PERSON HAS BEEN DESIGNED TO DO THE IMPOSSIBLE."

BILL JOHNSON

Children naturally learn and adapt to supernatural lifestyles. Present day culture exposes them to these things through fantasy, as in super-heroes, or through occult practices. When the people of God become proactive in training children in God's design, it helps to insure our children maintain their place in a life that is truly super, yet natural. This book plays an important role as it intentionally exposes them to miracle stories as the new norm. Our children were born for this purpose. Just as God partnered with David in his triumph over Goliath, so our children were designed to be able to take down the giants to their God-given destinies. Dick Joyce told us 40 years ago that "children do not have a junior Holy Spirit." Children naturally have a simple, uncomplicated faith in God. Keeping testimonies before them helps to anchor them in a relationship with a perfect Father who is always good. Let this book inspire you to establish the Christ-like supernatural life as the new norm for kids.

BILL JOHNSON

SENIOR LEADER, BETHEL CHURCH REDDING, CA

"LIKE ARROWS IN THE HAND OF A WARRIOR, SO ARE THE CHILDREN OF ONE'S YOUTH."

PSALM 127:4

I remember being in a church meeting when the speaker said, "Children don't have a junior Holy Spirit." As this phrase echoed through the building, an explosion of light entered my heart. "Of course! God doesn't give a little bit of Himself to kids, He gives ALL OF HIMSELF!"

One of the first times I saw this with my own eyes was when we had just moved to Redding, California, from Australia. I watched my two-and-a-half-year-old son, Zeke, be led by God to squat down in front of a dead plant and pray for it. As I watched him looking like a Jedi from Star Wars, I was thinking to myself, "What is he doing? Is he praying for that plant?" A few days later the dried up pepper tree came back to life and afterward outgrew two green peppers! After this amazing miracle in our family, I began to ponder on what the Lord was trying to show us. Zeke had never attended Bethel School of Supernatural Ministry, yet he was operating in God's power far more organically than I was.

In Matthew 18:3 Jesus says to his highly experienced ministry team, "Unless you are converted and become like little children, you will not enter the kingdom of heaven." He then echoes this message in Matthew 19:14 when he says, "Let the children alone and do not hinder them from coming to Me; for the kingdom of heaven belongs to such as these." It is imperative today that we understand our children are more connected to heaven's reality, and they are called to be active players in the advancement of his kingdom.

Sometimes in Christian life we can give children the message, "You guys stay over there and play, and let us adults do the real ministry over here." However, Jesus is raising up children in this hour to teach us to play and not be so serious, so that we can see an even greater move of God take place.

Just as Jesus doesn't give kids a junior Holy Spirit, he also doesn't give them a little "playroom in heaven" to keep them occupied. Wherever you live as you read these words, God has offered the entire kingdom of heaven to every child (Luke 12:32), and through them we will learn much about how heaven moves and brings dominion. As Solomon prophesied in Psalm 127:4, "Like arrows in the hand of a warrior, so are the children of one's youth."

Children are being raised up in families across the world as weapons that can destroy sickness, reverse poverty, and release heaven's abundance on earth. As you read this book, you will see children are alive and active in heaven's advancement. They, like us, are not perfect but are simply on a journey of pursuing the fullness of the kingdom. We hope this book stirs your heart and opens your imagination to pray that God unlocks the kids in your life (including the child in you) to step into the supernatural with Jesus. The kingdom is here and it's with the kids!

DAVE HARVEY

DIRECTOR, GLOBAL LEGACY & INCREASE PRODUCTIONS

CONTENTS

GLOSSARY OF TERMS

ACTIVATE: To encourage and teach others to practice their spiritual gifts and abilities in areas such as healing, prophecy, words of knowledge, encountering Father God, etc.

BSSM: Bethel School of Supernatural Ministry's mission is to equip and deploy revivalists who passionately pursue worldwide transformation in their God-given spheres of influence. Students are trained to continue in the ministry style of Jesus: to enjoy the presence of God, say what He is saying, and do what He is doing.

DECLARATION: Creative words spoken aloud by a Christian that bring about heaven's plans in a specific place or situation on earth.

FIRE TUNNEL: A prayer/blessing "tunnel" made of two lines of Christians facing each other who lay hands on and pray for people walking through the tunnel. The goal of a fire tunnel is to encounter God's presence.

HEALING ROOMS: Made famous by the revivalist John G. Lake, Healing Rooms are places where people from the community can come to encounter God's presence and receive healing through prayer from Christians.

INTERCESSOR: A Christian who releases God's joyous purpose into a specific place or situation on earth through prayer and declaration.

PROPHECY: A specific message from God to a person or group to strengthen, encourage, or comfort.

VISION: A spiritual reality seen with the mind's eyes. Often a picture or moving image.

WORD OF KNOWLEDGE: Specific details revealed by the Holy Spirit about another person's life.

01

FAMILY & HOME

RESURRECTING PLANTS!

DAVE HARVEY / CALIFORNIA, USA

One sunny California morning, I went outside under the patio to water my potted plants, which included some tomatoes, snow peas and a green pepper tree. Unfortunately, my past experience as a gardener hadn't been the greatest, as I would often see my plants die.

This morning when I went out, I was again confronted with this heartbreaking reality. The green pepper tree that I had planted had shriveled up a day or two earlier and now it was basically two dry sticks. Slightly annoyed, I stopped watering it and only watered the other plants around it.

While I was spraying the other plants, suddenly my two-and-a-half-year-old, Zeke, emerged from inside the house. He walked out, and without saying anything he squatted in front of the little plant that had shriveled up. Then he proceeded to stretch out his little hand like some Jedi warrior from Star Wars toward the dried up pepper tree.

Still holding the hose towards the other plants, I looked in wonder at my little man. "What is he doing? Is he praying for the plant?" After about 10 to 15 seconds of bending down arm stretched out, he popped up and walked off. In shock, I turned and said to him, "Hey Z, did you just pray for that plant?" I had never modeled praying for plants or taught him anything about anything like this. As only a little two-year-old can do, Zeke turned, look at me, and said, "Yeah," then jogged away.

One week later the little green pepper tree came back to life, and in the coming weeks it grew two green peppers! We celebrated God's goodness and how he used our little boy, despite never going to a school of supernatural ministry!

DREAM HOUSE

ARLEN & AARON / **UKRAINE**

O ur names are Arlen and Aaron. We're 13 and 10 years old, and this is a testimony of how we got our new house. We were already praying for a house for four years. We brothers were praying that it would be two stories high, our older sister Ariel was praying that it would be close to a forest or a field, our little sister Jasmine was praying that it would be pink, and our Dad was praying that it would have a garage and basement.

One night at a worship night, Aaron got touched by the Holy Spirit and talked with Jesus. Jesus asked Aaron, "Do you want a rich house, a medium house, or a poor house?" He answered, "I just want our daily bread."

After a month we got the house we prayed for. It was pink, was two stories high, had a garage and basement, and was near a forest and a field. God answers prayers!

BUNNY EYES

SCOTT BILIEUI / **CALIFORNIA, USA**

I was married with two children, but I was bound with lust and addiction, and I was being unfaithful to my wife. I kept it all secret, but I was deeply depressed.

At that time, my four-year-old son started attending Christian preschool, where his teacher had taught him the power of prayer. One day while I was in my room crying, my son walked in and asked, "Dad, what's wrong?" I had no words for him, and I didn't want to let the skeletons out of my closet. Undeterred by my lack of response, my little boy said to me, "Hey Dad, I think you should pray."

That night I cried out to the Lord, "Jesus, help me! Can you just help me?" Suddenly God reminded me of a memory from my childhood. I'd had a baby bunny who was born without eyes.

My mother was a woman of faith and said, "Son, in the Bible it says if you pray and ask God for anything and you believe that He will do it, then He will." That night I prayed, "I have no idea how to believe that you are going to do this, God, but I believe you will." The next day when I got up, the bunny had eyes! My mom went crazy and started telling everybody about it and telling me that I was going to be "the next healing evangelist called to the nations." I was embarrassed, and I refused to talk about it, locking the memory deep inside.

All I had received from church were laws I knew I couldn't fulfill. I didn't understand the Gospel, and I ended up moving away from God. So lying in bed that night 30 years later, praying the simple prayer my son told me to pray, I remembered the God who gave my blind bunny eyes to see. I said to myself, "I've made a mess of my life, but if you did that for me then, maybe you will save my family now."

In the following months, I told the truth to my wife. At first, she didn't want anything to do with me.

In the following weeks, I remembered a testimony I'd heard on Facebook six months prior where the pastor seemed

to speak directly to me, as if he knew my story. I decided to visit the church, and as I walked to the front with tears running down my face, a man stretched out his arms and lovingly asked me, "Are you ready to come home?" I let go of everything I had been trying to hang on to and surrendered it all to Jesus. In that moment, my life radically changed!

The days ahead were not easy, but in the midst of great brokenness, I would go out to my backyard and pray a simple prayer, "Jesus, I don't know what to do; help me." Every single day, the Lord would guide me step by step on how to clean up messes and make wrong things right.

I went to live with my mother, but I would still go home at night to tuck my kids in bed. My wife would usually leave as soon as I got there, but one night she stayed and asked me, "What did you do today?"

I started sharing what the Lord was doing in me. She asked me, "You are now on a spiritual journey with God. What about

me?" I told my wife the blind rabbit story. She was impacted but still needed answers on what to do next. I told her, "What I have learned from the Lord is that a man is supposed to lead his family, and I believe that if I lead and you follow, God is going to restore all of this."

Later I got a text from my wife, "Tonight I was brought to my knees in my living room, and I gave my life to the Lord." The following night when I went to tuck in my kids, my wife started reading Jesus' words from the Bible that we must forgive if we want to be forgiven. While she was reading, God immediately hit her heart with forgiveness. It didn't take years; addiction was broken. God's power and love came in and transformed our lives immediately, and we connected in a way that we had never connected in our previous seven years of marriage.

My wife and I went on to have more kids, and our whole family serves the Lord.

PARTNERING WITH ANGELS

BEC PHILLIPS / **AUSTRALIA**

We began carefully walking out this journey as a family to partner with heaven's angels, thanks to some amazing teaching we had been receiving at our church and a gift of seeing into the spirit realm, which was on one of our children. As adults, my husband and I couldn't really sense angels. But now we have learned to train our physical senses to discern them (Hebrews 5:14), and now my husband can feel a kind of buzz of energy on his body and in the air around him when an angel is present, kind of like the start of an orchestra playing. Now when the kids see an angel, they're helping us on this journey by letting us know, and together we ask God, "Jesus, what is the angel here for? Are they here for anyone in particular?"

One day we were in our living room and my youngest daughter Sara (five) said in a nonchalant way, "Oh, there's an angel there. It's always there. And it's right beside the fireplace." A little shocked and unable to physically see anything with our adult eyes, we thought we would check this out with our eldest son Jonah who has been able to see into this realm since he was little. I said, "Jonah, can you see anything?" Jonah kind of glanced around the corner and chimed, "Oh, yeah, there is, too!"

So now two of our kids could see the same angel. Jonah said that the angel was about the size of a man but like a shadow made out of light. According to what the kids have told us, angels can be different shapes and sizes. He described this angel as being like the outline of a person, but made up of light.

One of the other kids said, "Hey, why don't you ask what it's here for?" I thought, What a great idea! So we all asked Jesus. As an adult still learning how to interact with this realm, I felt peace, but I didn't say anything. A girlfriend who was with us and in the room also felt peace. Then Jonah exclaimed, "I know: peace and comfort!" So right there we had a confirmation that the angel was there to bring God's peace and comfort into our home.

I looked at Jonah and said, "We should release it, Jonah." So I said, "Okay, well, we release you to go and stand in the kids' bedroom." One of the boys hadn't been sleeping well for days, so we felt like this was a good idea.

Straight after this, Jonah said, "Ah, Mommy, the angel just walked down the hallway towards our bedroom." He watched it leave the living room and said it moved in something like picture frame motion, not fluently, but rather moving slowly in flashing images down the hall until it went into their bedroom.

The next morning our son who hadn't been sleeping well for days woke up and said, "I slept great last night, Mom!" We were ecstatic at how quickly God had answered a need in our family. After we partnered with heaven, the sleepless nights came to an end, and from that night onwards, all of our children slept in peace and comfort.

HER NAME IS BELLA

GABE VALENZUELA / **CALIFORNIA, USA**

When my son Judah was four years old, my wife Leah called me while I was at work one day and said, "Could you pick up a pregnancy test on the way home from work?" I was a bit shocked that she was telling me we were going to have a baby over the phone and asked, "Are you pregnant?"

"No, I don't think so," she said.

"So why do I need to get a pregnancy test?" I asked, confused.

Leah explained that earlier that day, Judah had randomly said to her, "Mom, you're pregnant, you're going to have a little girl, and you're going to call her Bella."

I got her a test, and sure enough, she was pregnant! When it came time to go to the doctor for a sonogram, we went as a family. The woman doing the sonogram said, "You're going to have a little girl." Leah and her mom started crying because we had two boys and were excited to have a girl! I excitedly looked at Judah, but the look on his face showed that he thought we were all dumb as if to say, "I told you this is what's happening."

Later on in the day I told Judah, "Come sit on the bed. Let's have a chat." At that point I knew Judah heard from the Lord, but I didn't know how accurately he heard.

I asked him, "How did you know that Mom was going to have a baby and that we should name her Bella?"

He looked at me and said, "The Lord told me."

I said, "I know, but how did He tell you? Was it really loud? Did you have a dream about it at night?"

Judah said, "Sometimes the Lord speaks real loud and you don't even have to pay attention. You just hear Him."

He got a big smile on his face. "Sometimes the Lord speaks really quiet, and you have to listen."

He became very excited and said, "Daddy, I really had to listen this time."

I was so excited about him hearing from the Lord, I grabbed his hand and asked him to pray for me!

PROPHETIC UPGRADES

DAVE HARVEY / CALIFORNIA, USA

I was standing outside in the heat of the day by our swimming pool on my day off when I suddenly heard God say to me, "Dave, why don't you pray for your boys?" I thought to myself, *Oh that's a great idea!* Then I kind of felt a bit bad for not regularly praying for them like my mum had prayed for me. But rather than beating myself up, I asked my Father, "What would you like me to pray?" Immediately, I felt Him say, "Pray that their prophetic gifts increase." So I said "Jesus, I pray that Zeke's, Jaden's and Chase's prophetic gifts increase."

The next day my eldest son Zeke came home from school and at the dinner table said, "Today the strangest thing happened. The teacher was pulling names out of a hat, and I would know the names before she pulled them out!" I looked at him excitedly, shocked at how quickly Jesus had answered my prayer. "Zeke, do you know what that is called?"

Zeke looked at me and said no. I said, "That's called a prophetic gift!" He smiled in wonder as I explained that I had just felt to pray for him and the boys about this the day before. This happened for Zeke three days running, where he was able to tell the future before it happened, and then we didn't hear much of it again.

A week later on the Friday before Father's Day, our six-year-old, Chase, raced around into the kitchen with a paper gift. "Here you go, Dad! Happy Father's Day!" he said with boldness. I looked at what seemed like a paper bracelet and said, "Thanks, Chase! Umm, what is it?" Without missing a beat, Chase said with confidence, "It's a watch, Dad! A watch!"

I smiled and thanked him and placed the paper bracelet on the shelf above my coffee machine. That night just as I was about to open Friday night service at Bethel, a man walked up to me and handed me a bright red Diesel watch! I couldn't believe it. It was my favorite brand and style! I didn't put two and two together until a week later when I was on the couch one night, and I heard God say, "You know Chase is operating in a prophetic gift when he's making things for you!"

Immediately, I remembered eight months earlier when Chase had walked into our house and handed me a green-roofed paper house that he had made in kids' church. In boldness he had said, "Here you go, Dad. It's a house for you!" As I sat on the couch, I remembered feeling God's presence in that moment and a seed of faith dropping into my heart, but after putting in on the fridge, I didn't think much more of it. Two weeks later, a friend had a dream and texted it to me. It said, "You and Taff took a risk and bought a house and then because it was so big and looked empty, people felt sorry for you and gave you money for furniture." A few weeks after that, the day we officially took over Global Legacy, Taff and I found the perfect house. We had no deposit saved and not an exciting credit score. With the help of some friends and some miraculous events, we got our first house in the USA! I was shocked as I remembered this and looked at my new red watch in my new house! Chase truly was prophesying the future like Zeke, but using paper models to do it!

13

ALWAYS LOVED

ANA STAFFORD / **CALIFORNIA, USA**

Eleven years ago, we adopted our sweet, precious daughter Emma from Romania. Her life is a miracle in itself.

When she was eight years old, she started asking me if I thought her birth mother loved her. Every time she asked I would answer, "Oh yes, I am sure she did, sweetie!" Since she kept asking the same question over and over again, I realized that my answer was not settling the pressing question of her heart, so I started praying that God would answer this question for her.

One day, she came home from Bethel Christian School, and as soon as she walked in the house, I knew something had happened. She sat me and my husband down and with big tears streaming down her face, she said:

"Today, during our soaking time in science, I had a vision. I saw myself as a baby in the arms of this young gypsy woman, and I knew she was my birth mother. She was wearing an orange shirt and a yellow flowy skirt. She looked almost Indian and her skin color was like mine... She was crying as she laid me in the crib and then walked away.

Then you and Daddy walked in. You came, picked me up, and held me so close. You were both crying, but your tears were of joy. You were so happy to take me home with you. Then I saw myself happily playing at the preschool in Texas, then at the preschool and YWAM base in Romania, then in third grade here in Redding.

I asked God why He was showing me all of that and taking me to all these places. He said, 'I want you to know that you have always been loved!'"

With tears streaming down her face, Emma looked up and said, "She loved me, too! She was sad to leave me, but I am so blessed to have you and Daddy be mine!" We all held each other and cried together for a long while, affirming our love

for her. Emma was completely overcome by God's love and intentionality to settle this pressing question of her heart in a way that only He could.

Jesus faithfully showed her all the people and places where she was loved. The picture to the right is one of the only pictures we have of her birth mother, wearing an orange shirt and a yellow skirt. Although we had told Emma her adoption story, we had not shown Emma the picture until after the encounter. "She is the one!" Emma said when she saw the picture of her birth mother for the first time. Emma is now eleven years old, and she has never asked that question again because deep in her heart, she knows that she has always been loved!

NEW KNEES

LINDA FOURIE / **SOUTH AFRICA**

My son, David, was diagnosed with Sensory Process Disorder, which caused his speech to be very slow and delayed.

I had knee pain ever since I was born. I eventually went to see a doctor, and after a scan, they diagnosed me with Patellofemoral Pain Syndrome. I stopped complaining about it or mentioning it to anyone because there was not much that the doctor could do, and after a lot of rehabilitation, the pain had not gone away.

One day, when David was three and a half years old, I went to pick him up from school. When we got home, we sat on the couch, and I asked him about his day. He looked at me and asked, "Mama, do you have an ouchie?" I said to him, "No, I don't have an ouchie," and asked him again about his day. However, he persisted in asking again if I had pain in my knee. Again I said no, but then I heard the Holy Spirit say, "Listen to him. There is something that I want to do." So I said, "Yes, Mama has an ouchie."

Without my showing him where, he stood up, walked right up to me and tapped my injured knee and asked if he could see. Then he rolled up my pants to just above my knee, and he put his hands on my knee. My husband and I can't actually remember ever teaching him how to pray for the sick, but he went straight into it. His hands felt like they were on fire! He then started talking to God, but I did not understand what he was saying. He finished talking and looked up at me, smiled, and walked away.

My knee felt really hot, and I felt like God said, "Test it!" So I decided to get up and check out if I had pain. Incredibly, for the first time I had no pain at all! I did a squat, and still I had no pain! My boy prayed for my healing, and I was completely healed! Maybe he was even speaking in tongues without my knowing!

Shortly after this miracle, David began to speak normally and was healed of Sensory Process Disorder.

17

JUMPING ON THE BED

DAVE HARVEY / **CALIFORNIA, USA**

We were at home, and Mum was out when I heard a terrible scream. I ran into our boys' bedroom only to find my eldest son Zeke hysterically crying, holding his knee. I asked what had happened, and he screamed that he'd fallen off of the bed after jumping. As I tried to console him, his younger brother Jaden was continuing to jump on the bed as if nothing had happened.

Then I had the thought that I should probably practice praying for him. So I said to Zeke, "Hey, let's pray to Jesus to heal your knee." Underneath his hollering cry, he obliged, so with not a ton of faith, I placed my hand on his little knee and prayed, "Jesus, I pray you take away all Zeke's pain." I looked up at him and said, "How is it Z? Any change?" He was still sobbing and said, "No, it's still sore!" I prayed again, but still there was no improvement. Then, in desperation, I thought to listen to Holy Spirit as to what we should do.

While I waited, a thought raced through my head: *Get Jaden to pray for him.* So I looked over at the three-year-old bouncing away while the scream opera was echoing around his room and said, "Jades, want to come and pray for your brother?" Sheepishly and after some encouragement, he obliged and walked over and placed his puffy little hand on Zeke's knee. "Jesus, heal Zeke's knee," said Jaden. Suddenly the crying stopped, and we looked up at Zeke. His eyes were wide open and too afraid to look down at his knee. He said, "Daddy, it's gone! It's gone! The pain's gone! The pain's gone!" We all celebrated with a sense of wonder! Jaden's prayer had worked!

"Jades, your prayer worked!" I shouted in relief. "Jesus healed Zeke's knee because you prayed!" We celebrated together our little miracle and how Jesus had stopped the knee pain. We had survived another accident without Mum yet again!

Effet

Effekt

Effect

02

SCHOOL

FORGIVING DAD

BECKY BABCOCK / ARGENTINA

Eleven-year-old Gabriela hurt her ankle and had to spend a week in her house while it healed. During this week she read two books that were required reading in a ministry school in Buenos Aires, Argentina, that her sister was attending: *When Heaven Invades Earth* by Bill Johnson and *Love Says Go* by Jason Chin.

After reading the books, Gabriela was really excited and started doing activations from *Love Says Go*. She saw a classmate at school named Lucas, who always looked sad, so she started talking to him. She found out that he was very angry at his father, who had abandoned his family. Gabriela told Lucas that it was really important that he forgive his father. Between classes, they talked throughout the day, and finally Lucas decided to forgive his dad.

Prompted by the Holy Spirit, Gabriela then asked Lucas if he needed healing in his body. He said that there was a part of his rib that was missing from birth. She prayed for him a few times and then he went to the restroom to see if anything had changed. He came back totally shocked and said that he could now feel the part of his rib that had previously been missing! Lucas was amazed and said, "This is so crazy. Five minutes ago I was an atheist, but now I believe in God."

Gabriela then noticed that he was wearing glasses and asked him why he had to wear them. Lucas told her he had a disease in his eyes that caused one eye to be blurry and one eye to have tunnel vision, giving him constant headaches. Each year he had to have surgeries on his eyes, but they hadn't been able to correct the problem.

Gabriela prayed once, and his headache disappeared. She prayed again, and he felt something like fire in his eyes. She then told him to pray for his own eyes, and the blurriness and tunnel vision left. He went to his eye doctor a week later, and his doctor said that his eyes were fine, and he no longer needed surgery.

JOHN THE BAPTIST

KONRAD JANZEN / BRAZIL

We listened to teaching at Bethel that there was no "junior Holy Spirit" for children and that the same Holy Spirit resides in them, with the same amount of power. We believed that, but we hadn't yet seen it played out.

When we went to meet with our son Johann's school teacher, the teacher told us that our son led people to Jesus. I asked, "How can that be real in a three or four-year-old kid?"

The teacher then told us about a day in the classroom when worship time was ending and they were transitioning into storytelling time. Johann said, "Jesus is here, Teacher." His classmate said, "I'm not feeling it." But Johann told the classmate to just say, "Come, Holy Spirit." All the students spoke those words out, and a big move of God began to happen in the classroom. The teacher felt the Holy Spirit moving, so she asked, "Who else is feeling this or seeing this? Who doesn't feel it?" Then with Johann, she led the whole class to invite Jesus into their lives.

If I had been the teacher I would have said, "Yes, Jesus is here. Now let's move on to story time." But hearing this story, we learned that the Holy Spirit uses and even invites little children to follow His leading.

Afterwards, we remembered a prophetic word we'd received about Johann before we were pregnant with him. The prophetic word was that he would be like John the Baptist, preparing the way for people to come to the Lord. Johann means John, and his last name is Baptist in Portuguese! God showed us that we don't have to wait for our son's calling to begin when he is an adult, but that it is for each day, for right now, even as he's a child.

Today our kids do ministry with us and pray for people at their school here in Brazil. They have words of knowledge, and people are healed when they pray for them!

JESUS KNOWS MY NAME!

MICHAELA GENTILE / CALIFORNIA, USA

I teach at Bethel Preschool a class of four- and five-year-old children. One day the kids in my class were being a little wild. After giving them some stretches, I had them lie down and take deep breaths. Once they were relaxed, I had them close their eyes and imagine the following:

You're walking through a beautiful green field. You can smell the wildflowers that grow all around you. There is a gentle breeze and the sun warms your skin. And then you hear someone say your name. You look around but can't see anyone. The voice calls again, so you follow the sound up a hill, and when you get to the top, you see in front of you the most beautiful castle you've ever seen. The voice calls your name from inside the castle.

The children then followed the voice all the way into the castle to find Jesus, the King. He then led them in a tour of the castle, showing them different rooms.

Usually when I lead these activities, the children are wiggling and not very engaged. But this time all the children took their time before opening their eyes and sitting up. Some children remained lying down for a few minutes after other children were up.

Then some began to talk about what they had seen. One boy from Germany, who had spent most of the year not speaking English, was wide-eyed as he raised his hand to share, "Teacher, Jesus said my name! Jesus said my name!" He said this over and over as if he couldn't believe that Jesus actually knew who he was and had called out his name. My co-teacher and I looked at each other with tears because of his passion.

We told his parents about what had happened and they shared that, unbeknownst to us, two nights prior they had been reading to him from the Bible about Samuel and Eli when God called Samuel by name. He had told his parents that he wanted to hear God say his name like Samuel had. So in this encounter with Jesus, he heard Him say his name!

When his dad asked him, "What does God's voice sound like?" the son replied, "Like many waters."

FIRE TUNNEL OUTPOURING

CARA WINSPEAR / CALIFORNIA, USA

I'm a teacher at Bethel Christian School. After a school pep rally, some parents of students arranged a fire tunnel. Students went through the tunnel as parents prayed for them, then joined the tunnel to pray for their peers. The tunnel was long, and the presence of the Lord was thick.

While we laughed and staggered our way back to the classroom, two of my students were giggling in the Spirit and couldn't stop. They asked if we could continue pressing in to God, so I played keys while the class soaked and worshiped.

Five minutes before recess, one girl asked if she could invite the other 6th grade class into our classroom, and I said yes. Fifteen to twenty students stayed in from recess to continue enjoying the Lord's presence.

The Lord showed me a mental image of a child receiving prayer and falling under the power of the Holy Spirit, so I shared the picture with the class, and we began asking the Lord to fill up individuals He highlighted. As we did this, they encountered God in different ways, and many fell under the power of the Spirit and were caught by classmates.

The atmosphere was electric with God's presence. The students were flowing with the Lord, and I no longer directed anything. Many students were weeping and crying out for more of the Lord. Others were lying on the ground, oblivious to everything. Some were dancing with flags and others were praying together.

By lunchtime many children stayed in the room, not even stopping to eat. Throughout the afternoon, more than half the school came through the room to experience this outpouring of the Holy Spirit.

It was breathtaking to see tiny kindergarteners lying there, shaking under the power of the Spirit, alongside big sixth-graders who were crying out for more of God, and eighth-graders who prayed silently, heads bowed to their knees as they connected intimately with the Father.

One kindergarten student had returned to his class but asked his teacher, "Can I go back upstairs and keep talking to Jesus?" Another student yelled out, "There is no sickness where God is, so all sickness has to leave this room right now!" and prayed for many individuals' healing. I prayed with two girls who began to speak in tongues for the first time. Receiving the gift of tongues was a turning point for one of the girls who began to let go of negative mindsets and believe her identity in God. This beautiful outpouring lasted more than four hours, and we are forever marked by it!

NO HOLDING BACK

CARA WINSPEAR / CALIFORNIA, USA

One day in chapel at Bethel Christian School (BCS), principal Don Mayer shared that God is both Savior and Judge. He asked the kids to consider whether they had asked God to forgive them of their sins and be their Lord and if they were living in a way that reflected the seriousness of Jesus' sacrifice for us.

I'm a sixth grade teacher at BCS, and when we returned to class to discuss the sermon from the morning, many of my students expressed a desire to say a full yes to the Lord. I felt that God wanted me to lead the students in a time of repentance. I had them get out their journals and write about anything that was holding them back from God. I also asked them to tell God what they were specifically sorry for, and then to write what God said in response, since repentance is changing the way you think. They took it very seriously and wrote for a long while.

I had a sense that next God wanted to do a divine exchange. I asked them to stand and imagine they were holding the things they were repenting of in their hands. Then together we lifted our hands over our heads, symbolically releasing those things to God. Next, I had the students keep their hands open to receive the gift He wanted to give in return.

I felt that the students were meant to pray for one another, so I instructed them to do so. They gathered in groups to pray for their friends, and I have rarely seen a group of students so quickly connect to the Lord as they did. I believe the doorway of repentance led them directly into God's presence.

As the students prayed for one another, a number of them fell under the power of the Spirit and were caught by their peers. Some cried, others laughed, and still others lay on the floor shaking in His presence. One student belly laughed for 45 minutes. Led by Holy Spirit, we asked the Lord to give her the gift of tongues, and she received a beautiful prayer language with incredible ease.

It was so beautiful to see these students' hunger and how God met them so powerfully!

03

OUT & ABOUT

CLEARING OUT A HOSPITAL

HANNAH SCARBOROUGH / SOUTHEAST ASIA

My husband grew up in Southeast Asia, where his parents are still in full-time ministry. Throughout his childhood he witnessed the supernatural on a daily basis, and many miracles occurred around him. Despite being nominally Christian, the region still had deep roots in animism, with witch doctors practicing voodoo and other dark occult practices. But a few years ago, the island, so full of pain, fear, and spiritual bondage, started experiencing full-on revival!

On the base lived local children who had been brought out of abusive, neglectful, or poverty-stricken households and placed in family homes with local parents. There was also a hospital ward on the base, which served the local community. One day, the children were encouraged to enter the hospital ward and pray for the patients. They did so joyfully and afterwards went back to school or whatever they were up to that day.

The next day, my mother-in-law walked up to the ward to check on the patients, as was often her habit. The only patient remaining was a physiotherapy patient. The rest were completely healed and had checked out and gone home! She was completely shocked and amazed. How good is our God? In one day, using children, He cleared out the entire ward!

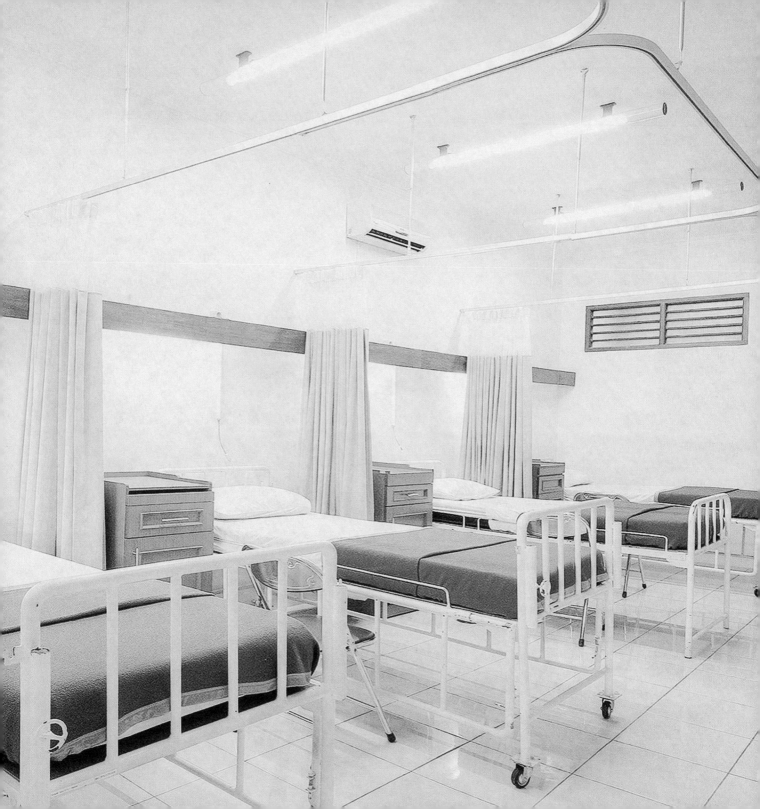

A DAUGHTER'S HUG

DAVE HARVEY / CALIFORNIA, USA

After seeing my boys begin to grow in their prophetic gifts in their everyday lives, I felt to activate them further. I had been asked by a friend to speak at her ministry, Hope Recovery, an incredible team that provides men and women with encounters with Jesus so they can walk in freedom from addiction to alcohol and drugs.

I called my three boys together, Zeke (11), Jaden (8) and Chase (5). I asked them to make a Lego model for someone, and ask Jesus what color clothing they were wearing and what He wanted to say to them. Because it was later at night, my eldest son Zeke brought the models and joined me to minister to these wonderful people. It was amazing to release the words and the Lego models together. Every person was touched by Jesus powerfully. Then it was Zeke's turn. God had given him the color purple and he pointed to a lady wearing purple, who was sitting on the front row. Earlier, she had shared with the entire group that her daughter had been taken to prison for five years.

After Zeke pointed to her, she came up and stood with us in front of everyone. He gave her his Lego spaceship and said to her, "The next time you see your daughter, she's going to run towards you, give you a big hug and be smiling." As he said the words, I felt something rush across from Zeke and hit the lady, kind of like a wind. I couldn't believe it! Instantly, this beautiful grandmother began to cry as God touched her heart and gave her hope! What we didn't know was that this elderly lady was now the sole care provider for her daughter's young girl.

A week later our friend came over. "You've got to hear this!" She reported that the grandmother had woken up the next morning, and her granddaughter had walked up to her to say, "Grandma, did you get a word last night from a man?" The grandmother was completely shocked, "Yes I did, honey! How did you know?" The little girl replied, "Oh, I know, Grandma, because I had a dream last night, and in the dream I saw the boy give you a word, and God told me that mom was going to be okay."

One week later, the little girl's mother was suddenly released from prison after being sentenced with a three- to five-year term! The grandmother was shocked when she got a knock on the door and her lost daughter rushed in and hugged her, just as Zeke had said.

ADVENTURES WITH BOYS

RICK CHAVEZ II / CALIFORNIA, USA

We love releasing the Kingdom with our sons as we go about our everyday lives.

One time we were at Denny's, so we asked our boys to pray and ask Holy Spirit if there was anything He would like to do or say to our waitress. Both my wife and I and one of our sons, Seth, felt the Lord wanted to bless her because she was struggling financially. Our youngest son, Ricky, heard that her heart was sad because someone had died and that God wanted to encourage her. He said, "Look at her face. You can tell that someone died, and it's sad." Both my wife and I thought that might be a stretch.

When the waitress returned to our table, we asked if we could pray for her and encourage her. Then we blessed her with some money that we all agreed upon giving her and told her that Jesus loved her. In response she told us that she woke up that morning feeling sad in her heart because a year ago to the day her sister had died in a car accident. She said that when her sister passed away, she and her sister had unresolved conflict, so she had not had a chance to make peace in their relationship.

After we prayed with her, she said she felt better and uplifted because God heard her prayer and sent a family to come in and encourage her. She said she could now forgive herself and saw how much God cares for her.

Another day we saw a homeless man who could barely stand trying to hold himself up with a cane and assistance from a friend. We felt that our boys, Seth and Ricky, were to pray for him. We asked his permission for our children to pray for him, and he said yes! As the boys laid hands on him and prayed for healing, he wept uncontrollably.

After praying, they asked if he felt any better. He informed us that he was full of pain before they prayed, but after they prayed, he had no pain! He lifted his cane in the air and was walking back and forth crying, saying he had not been able to do that on his own for months!

We love going on adventures with our sons. There is no "junior Holy Spirit."

NUEVA VIDA

KARA WESTERMANN / NICARAGUA

PART I

For the last six years, I have been in Nicaragua, and I live beside the Nueva Vida Trash Dump. "Nueva Vida" means "new life." My heart is to empty out every trash dump because no human deserves to live in a trash dump. The dump is full of fumes, biowaste and other hazards. Typically, the children do not want to leave the dump because it is all they know. Their friends are there, and they feel free to run around and ride about in trucks and search for food. My focus is that we would be able to relocate the most vulnerable from the dumps first: elderly, babies, widows, pregnant moms and small children. One little girl has only one relative: her grandmother, for whom she forages to buy life-saving medicine. In spite of the great need, we help one person at a time.

A few months ago, I was in Mark Brooks' BSSM class called His Glory and His Presence. At one point, one of the BSSM pastors, Richard Gordon, stopped the class and called out three people in the room. He said, "Stand up because the power of God is going to fall on you." I stood up, and the moment I did, my whole body got burning hot. I started shaking, and waves of power hit me. I wept because I could see images of the children in the trash dump running towards me like a movie scene. I thought to myself, *My heart is for them. If I'm going to get power, it's to see their lives changed.* I had an amazing encounter in the class and went back to our main session, and we entered into worship. In class I take notes on my phone. Usually, I do not get cell service in the main sanctuary, but that day I did.

Suddenly, my phone began to vibrate as I received lots of photos and messages. My team from Nicaragua was sending me messages of a sudden outpouring of the Holy Spirit on the children in the dump. The pictures showed children lying on the ground in His presence. In the past we had already seen testimonies from another trash dump, where children went into visions of Jesus, were taken into heaven and shortly afterwards were invited onto national television to tell the nation of Nicaragua what Jesus had done in their lives. However, this had never happened in Nueva Vida! Some of the children reported that they went to heaven, while others had visitations from Jesus.

Some of the kids live with us at our base in Nicaragua while others live at home. The day the Holy Spirit crashed on them, they did not go home. The team could not get them to leave, so their parents came to pick them up, and they also began to fall flat on their faces under the power of the Holy Spirit. One of the dads slid down the door frame and fell on the floor. One child's older sister fell flat on her face. One boy had an out-of-body experience, and others got baptized in the Spirit.

The other trash dump had been a harder atmosphere with lots of drugs and heaviness. We had been contending to see God crash in there. After I got all those voicemails and texts, I asked when it had happened. We traced the time back, and it was the exact time that Richard had stopped the class, and the Holy Spirit had fallen on me! Somehow, while I was in California being hit by God's presence, at the same time it was falling on the kids in the dump!

NUEVA VIDA

KARA WESTERMANN / NICARAGUA

PART II

One little girl, Ruth, had a lot of walls up. She was angry, hurting and disruptive. She wanted to hit other kids and only came to us because she liked our dance class. We would do beautiful, choreographed dances to worship music. Outside of dance class, it was difficult to have her there. She refused to be touched or hugged.

When the Holy Spirit fell on the Nueva Vida dump in October, Ruth was especially touched. Her encounter lasted the longest. She drew a picture of a heart with herself inside it. Jesus told her she lived inside of His heart.

I returned to Nicaragua over Christmas, and the Holy Spirit crashed again on the kids. Ruth was out the longest. We lay on the ground, and I held her in my arms as she cried and cried. As I was lying there on the ground with her, the Holy Spirit said to me, "I want you to get up and go to her house because today is the day her mom gives her life to me."

I asked her if her mom was home and if we could visit her. With another team member, I went to her house. Her mother is a single mom with six kids. She was also angry and hurting like Ruth.. I introduced myself to her and told her that Ruth had just had an incredible encounter with the Holy Spirit. This was two months after the first encounter. Her mother said, "Yeah, my daughter is totally different."

I said, "Yes, that is Jesus. And while the Holy Spirit was touching us today, Jesus spoke to me about you. Jesus told me to come to you because today is the day you are going to give your life to Him."

She burst into tears. You could almost feel the weight coming off of her, and you could feel His peace. In her home, a rusted-out, tin shack beside a trash dump, the Holy Spirit came down in peace. We led her to the Lord. I could tell they are not a touchy-feely family, but as soon as Ruth's mom gave her life to the Lord, Ruth came running, and they held each other.

It was the moment we had been contending for: to see families restored. Because of the change in Ruth, her mom had now opened up to Jesus.

PERFECT EYES

MICHAEL MCMACKEN / ARIZONA, USA

I went with my wife and my four sons on our Christmas break to meet my retired brother and his wife in Quartzsite, Arizona. They would go there to escape the harshness of the winter in their motor home joining thousands of others. But while we were there, my sister-in-law Melody had a stroke and was rushed to the hospital. She spent the night, and upon her return she could not see well. Her eyes were crossed and unable to focus. My brother asked us to pray. When I was in their motor home looking at Melody, I had no faith for her to be healed.

But then suddenly out of my 13-year-old son Samuel came a faith-filled declaration, "Aunt Melody, God is going to make your eyes better than they have been before!"

The next day Melody's eyes were no longer crossed! As she was trying to read her book, she could not focus, but then she took her glasses off, and she found she could read perfectly. In one night, after the declaration of our son, God had made her eyes better than they were before!

HEALED AT IN-N-OUT

SYDNEY GRACE WORTH / CALIFORNIA, USA

'm eight and we had been reading the Increase books at home, learning about how God can use ordinary people to help others get healed. Well, I met an outstanding woman called Susan at a conference with two amazing speakers, Mel Tari and Chad Dedman. She is in her 70s and so nice and hard-working. I was talking to her, and the next day when I asked my dad to go to In-'N-Out, I saw her sitting by herself.

I went around the people and came up to her without my dad because I knew I could do it on my own. I started to talk to her because I love to talk to people, and asked if she needed prayer for anything. She said she did, for her knee. So I started praying and she was saying, "Yes, Lord," while closing her eyes. I was saying, "Thank you, Lord, for Susan. Thank you for healing her knee. Thank you for loving her and letting her love you, Lord."

Afterwards, I asked how her knee felt. I asked, "50 percent, 80, 90 or 100 percent?" She said it was 80 percent so I prayed more, and the same thing happened. When I was finished, I heard a crack! And I said, "Did you hear that?" She said yes!

I asked which percent it was at now, and she said 100. We hugged each other like 30 times! She said so many people had prayed for her, but her leg had never been healed. And then she started crying. She also needed prayer for her sleep. My dad came over and prayed for that, and I prayed, too. God can definitely do miracles! He used me and He can use you.

KIDS

WORSHIPING WARRIORS

JOSHUA & RACHAEL MINTER / SOUTH AFRICA

We started our week in East London, South Africa, with the news that a man had been brutally murdered by many people in the rubbish dump community of our missions base with Global Mercy Missions. Our children had witnessed it, and afterwards, we noticed that our preschoolers were reenacting what they had witnessed, pretending to beat each other up. For some children, it was their own parents who participated in the murder. The atmosphere was thick with violence and strife.

Horrified and broken, I turned to Holy Spirit and asked Him how to respond. He told me to worship with the children. So I led the children in a local song worshiping the Holy Spirit, and He started to move in such a mighty way that every child was on his or her face weeping and wailing in the presence of the Lord. This continued for over an hour, and not one child was distracted with what was happening around him or her. We could see the trauma leaving the children with every tear. This outpouring of the Holy Spirit continued for two weeks. Every day the children would gather together to worship the Holy Spirit, which manifested in weeping and grieving.

But one day I woke up and said, "Holy Spirit, I don't think I can handle listening to my children cry again. Their cries are breaking my heart. When are you going to reveal yourself as a happy God? When are you going to bring the joy of your presence? I am grateful for how you have moved, but Holy Spirit, I know there is more to your nature than what these children are experiencing."

The Holy Spirit's response shifted our reality. He said, "My son, when will you show them that I am a happy God? When will you reveal Me as the One who makes you glad?" So, full of courage, I wrote a song with the children in their own language, saying, "The Holy Spirit makes me laugh, the Holy Spirit makes me dance, the Holy Spirit makes me cry."

The Holy Spirit showed up once again, but in a new way! The children danced upon the same ground that they had cried on. They were filled with joy and laughter in the same place that they had been healed from their trauma. They rolled around screaming with the joy of the Lord. Bear in mind, they had no reference to that kind of manifestation of the Holy Spirit. They had never seen that before.

Their laughter was so loud that the parents and the community members came to find out what was happening. As they walked into the room, they were moved by His presence.

As a result, the community justice (murder) has come to a halt, with very few cases of violence and crime taking place. Since the outpouring on that day, many people have gotten saved and left their old lives behind. The changing of the tides has begun, and it started with our children receiving the baptism of the Holy Spirit!

COOKIES & CASTLES

KARA WESTERMANN / NICARAGUA

Our children's pastor, Ingrid, is a first-year realtor and was blessed to sell more homes in the month of December than all other 78 agents in her office through the favor of the Lord. However, she had one client who had been experiencing blockage after blockage with completing the sale for some time. The process was very time-consuming, and frustration was growing all around.

At our church's holiday gathering, the teacher, Bill, was sharing about honoring others and the Lord through gifts. Bill had a Christmas cookie decorating kit and asked the children to pray, asking the Lord whom they could honor with a decorated cookie and encouraging word. After hearing Jesus reveal a name, the children set about decorating their cookies with great excitement. When all budding artists had completed their edible masterpieces, Bill put on quiet soaking music and asked the children to journal what they were seeing and hearing for the person they chose to honor.

One of the students, an eight-year-old named Samantha, felt to honor our children's pastor. She presented her the cookie and shared her journal entry, which read, "There is some kind of problem at work you have been working on, and Papa God said that it's going to get all worked out." Four days later, the issue with the sale resolved, and after five months, it is closing!

04

CARS, PARKS & FUN

KNOCKOUT PUNCH!

DAVE HARVEY / AUSTRALIA

We had arrived at a park to meet one of our friends. After parking the car we walked up the sidewalk and saw her approaching with another young mom and her two daughters. After a quick hello hug, she asked if we would mind praying for her friend, who desperately needed a miracle. The young mother had Fibromyalgia.

I looked at the two girls standing beside their mother, got down low and felt to tell them the testimony of a man in Mexico whose knees and hips were healed. I told them how God had led me to ask three young men who didn't know Jesus to pray for a man who was on crutches with bandaged knees. After telling them that Jesus was healing everyone, I had the men place their hands on this cripple, one after the other and say, "Jesus, heal him." As these young men followed my lead, Jesus instantly healed the man's knees and hips, and he was able to walk without crutches! I could see the little girls' eyes getting bigger as faith entered their hearts. I asked, "Would you like to heal Mom, just like these men healed this man?" They said yes.

So they put their hands on their mom and prayed a simple, childlike prayer, "Jesus, please heal Mom!" Before they even finished, she crashed onto the grass as if someone had thrown a punch at her! No one had touched her, but she lay on the grass shaking and trembling. I quickly asked her if she was okay. As she trembled under God's power, she looked at us with a slight smile and assured us she was fine. We all stood in awe as Jesus did his work.

The next day at church, when we were sharing testimonies, the young mother stood up and shared her miracle. "Yesterday my girls prayed for me, and last night I had the first full night of sleep in over two years! I woke up this morning completely pain free, and I can also now raise my arms for the first time without pain!" Jesus knocked her Fibromyalgia right back to hell in a public park, and He used two of His secret weapons to do it!

MOMMY'S SHOULDER

TINA MILLER / CALIFORNIA, USA

Years ago, I was in a skiing accident and messed up my shoulder. The doctors never really gave a diagnosis for it, but it was constantly hurting and popping when I'd rotate my shoulder. That was accompanied by a burning sensation.

Then a few years later, I dislocated my shoulder, which made the existing condition worse. One night I was at our small group, and everyone prayed for my shoulder. It started feeling better, and when I moved my shoulder, it wasn't popping as much. On the way home from small group, I was praying for complete healing and just thanking God for what He had done already.

My two-and-a-half-year-old daughter, Aliyah, asked me if my shoulder hurt. I said yes. She asked if she could pray for it and said, "Dear God, thank you for Mommy's shoulder. In Jesus' name. Amen." Instantly, through the simple prayer of my little daughter, God completely healed my shoulder!

THE SANDPIT AND THE SEARCHER

ANONYMOUS / UNDISCLOSED

We were living overseas in a closed-access country to the Gospel. I would take my two-year-old son to the nearby sports field to play in the sand pile. The sports field was a part of the local university, and the students on a nice weather day would come to sit on the field to enjoy the sunshine.

In the midst of my son playing in the sand pile one day, he decided to suddenly stop what he was doing and run onto the field, passing a number of students until he stopped in front of a girl sitting by herself in the middle of the field. As most local people do, she tried to offer him a treat. I ran to catch up to him, only to notice that the girl was reading the Bible.

I was able to engage her in conversation and discovered this was her first time ever to read the Bible. I asked her if she knew where to begin reading since it was her first time, and she explained that the person who gave her the Bible hadn't given her any instructions. I explained to her about the Old Testament and New Testament, gave her suggestions on where to begin reading, and encouraged her in her pursuit of truth.

My son continued to play while I stood stunned, wondering how he knew to stop playing and run directly to this young lady!

DRIVING WITH PROPHETS

CAL PENNO / NEW ZEALAND

The first prophetic word I received when I came to Bethel in 2015 was that God was already speaking to me through my kids, but it was going to increase. Since then my two sons walk in the supernatural. To be honest, the Lord speaks to them first about what is going to happen in our lives, and they are the ones that come and tell us about it.

I was recently driving and talking on speaker phone to a friend who had just attended a prophetic conference at Bethel. My son Will, who is nine, interrupted me, saying he wanted to give her a word, and I told him, "Just wait. Mommy's on the phone." Finally I was saying goodbye, and Will said, "I need to talk to her!" so I let him.

Will told my friend, "I have a word for you. l saw you standing before a lot of people preaching the Word. You carry breakthrough, and as you spoke, people were being healed and set free. You will be going to other nations to bring this Word." My friend started crying, and I was thinking, Oh no, she didn't like the word or something. But she said, "No, Cal, this is exactly the same word I got at Bethel during the prophetic conference!"

Then my four-year-old son Izaak chimed in, "God is telling me to tell you that He loves you so much." We were amazed.

Another day while driving, I saw a very black spirit across the road where I was waiting for a train to pass. I was praying and binding it. One minute later, my son Will, who was eight, said, "Mom, what does Satan look like?" I said I thought he must be black and not good-looking. Will said, "I can see him, and I'm telling him he's not going to catch me because I'm with Jesus."

One day at church I was going through a difficult time, and a lady who meant well was actually killing my faith by telling me that what I was praying for was impossible. I left and said to Will, who was six, "What type of faith do you want to have?" He looked at me and said, "Mom, I want to have the type of faith that I can take risks." I felt like he was prophesying to me! So I said that was the type of faith I was going to have, and I carried on, forgetting about the lady's discouragement. And then what the lady told me was impossible began to happen!

YOUNG ENTREPRENEUR

DAVE HARVEY / CALIFORNIA, USA

My son Zeke had a dream to own a trampoline. After I talked with him about the power of business, he was ready to start one (at age five). So we prayed for a "God-idea" or an opportunity to arise.

A few weeks later we were at our friends' home, which they had recently bought, and they were talking about their new landscaping, in particular removing a ton of bark. After talking with Zeke, we realized that this could be an opportunity. So after a conversation with our friends, and a handshake at one dollar per wheelbarrow, Zeke was ready to start his first business.

The days were 115°F (46°C) so we had to be at work around 6am. Zeke had managed to recruit some help by convincing his two friends to help him fill the wheel barrows. So with a little help from me, Zeke and his friends went at it with shovels and dust pans. After about a week of early morning starts, Zeke was ready to finish his business, having earned $45 cash. He paid his friends with candy from the store, and was left with $40 to put towards his trampoline.

A new trampoline was about $250, and Zeke wondered how we would ever earn enough. So we prayed some more. Then one day my wife was searching Craigslist (an online community selling platform in the USA) and she found a brand new trampoline (still in the box) without the mat for $40! We couldn't believe it, and although it wasn't a complete trampoline, we felt to go for it. We called the man, confirmed the price and went and picked up the 1/2 trampoline for the exact amount he'd earned from his business!

The mat (as you know) is quite important; however, after seeing God provide the first stage of this miracle, we were expectant that he had some more surprises for us.

While we waited for clues on what to do next, little did we know that an amazing young man in our community had heard about Zeke's business and trampoline dream. Without telling us, he had told the story to his friends and family and started a fundraiser for people to give money towards the mat to realize the trampoline dream. Within a week, this young man had raised over $150 and surprised Zeke! We all were astounded at this young man's kindness, and we couldn't believe how God had worked this dream out.

This trampoline has lasted our family over seven years and still is a place of endless fun and memories at our home. I pray that Jesus gives business ideas and favor to every kid out there who has a dream!

CASH FOR CLOTHES

HANNAH GIDDENS / CALIFORNIA, USA

My son has a beautiful, sweet faith in Jesus. I often walk into his room and find him reading his Bible. He does get a prize when he finishes it, but it's much deeper than that!

He came home from school the other day with a $100 bill. When I asked him about it, his simple reply was, "I found it just off the path when I went for a walk in the forest with my class, which is great because I prayed to God for some money for clothes, and now I have some!"

In my head immediately came so many questions: Should you have handed it in to someone? Did you tell your teacher? Whose could it be? Those questions are still there in my head, but I didn't feel to deal with them right then!

What I was touched by was his confident faith in His Father to provide. He was in need (he really does need clothes)! He asked, and he received. For him, there were no questions. The expectation for him was for God to come through for him! So much I can learn from this sweet-hearted boy!

HERE BIRDIE!

GABE VALENZUELA / CALIFORNIA, USA

One day I was in the backyard at my in-laws' house with my son Judah, who was about three years old and talking a little. As Judah sat on my lap, we watched a hummingbird flying around nearby. Judah got excited and said, "Birdie, birdie!" But then the hummingbird flew away over a fence, and Judah started to cry that it had left. I didn't know what to do. I tried to comfort him saying, "It's OK, it'll be back," but it didn't come back.

Then, not thinking, I said, "Hey, just tell the hummingbird to come back." I was just trying to get him to do something else instead of crying. He put out his hand and said, "Come here, birdie! Come here, birdie!" Just then six or more hummingbirds flew together over the fence! In my life I've never seen more than two hummingbirds together. They flew around for 15 seconds, long enough to make him very happy and excited. He was clapping and saying, "Birdie, birdie!"

My mother-in-law had been watching from the kitchen window and came out saying, "Did you see that? Did you see all those hummingbirds?" I answered, "Yep, I saw them. I can't believe it, but I saw them," and told her what had happened.

For me this was a beautiful experience of the love of the Lord to fulfill a little child's desire. It wasn't like he was injured, and it wasn't anything serious, but he was definitely sad. And God cared about that

GOLDEN

CHRIS & PRISCILLA JONES / CALIFORNIA, USA

Our church, The Father's House, was planted with 13 adults and 30 children. From the beginning, God told us the children would lead the way in a touch from God, and they would show us how to be childlike if we would honor them.

This past summer was really difficult for our church leadership, but at the same time, kids were coming to the altar and worshiping, getting lost in the presence of the Lord, weeping, praying for each other, and getting filled with the Holy Spirit without anyone laying hands on them.

One day during worship, my six-year-old son got gold dust all over his hands—something I didn't have a grid for at the time. He waved and shook his hands, blowing on them, not knowing what it was. He kept saying his hands were tingling and felt like they were on fire, and there were little "sparkles" all over them. He asked me to hold him and not let him go because he thought he was going to fall over.

The next week during worship he stared at the ceiling as if he was seeing something for a minute. Then he said he had seen a very big statue of Jesus in the middle of the church with a strong whirlwind going around and around Him. He said, "Then the tornado sucked up all the hurt and pain into the sky, and everyone was then able to praise and celebrate Jesus." He was almost euphoric.

Then he noticed the sparkles on his hands again. He told me, "Dad, look at your hands. They have sparkles on them." I was amazed to see I had them on my hands, too. He then said to me, "Daddy, if you get on the stage right now and tell everyone to look at their hands, they'll have sparkles all over them too!"

For some reason, I didn't do it. I think I felt worried about what the people in the church would think. However at the end of the service, five people came up who didn't know anything about my son's encounter, and each shared how they also had gold sparkles all over their hands.

That same evening when we got home from church, my wife admitted that she was a little skeptical. She began asking the kids if they had done any crafts in children's church that might have involved gold glitter, but they had not. As she took off our son's shoes and socks, she was shocked to see that he also had the sparkles on the tops and bottoms of his feet!

I shared this with a few people at a restaurant after a service when the "sparkles" were no longer on my son's hand. As I shared, it started manifesting on a couple of people in the parking lot! We were all laughing and crying and praising God. This manifestation of gold dust continued for two or three weeks, and it all started with the children!

69

05

CHURCH

EMPTYING A WHEELCHAIR

LUKE SCOTT / **ENGLAND**

My younger brother was ten years old when he went to England to a big outreach event. He saw fifty people gathered around a lady in a wheelchair praying for her to get healed. But as time went by, they gradually stopped, gave up, and walked away. My little brother was not happy with that and said, "That's not right. She is supposed to come out of that wheelchair!"

He looked the lady in the eye and told her, "God says you are supposed to walk." He had her attention, and she was ready to follow his lead. He grabbed her hand, pulled her out of the wheelchair, and said, "In Jesus' name, walk!" And he started walking her around the room seven times. On the seventh time, she was not just walking, but she was running, and she picked up the wheelchair and threw it in the trash!

When I asked my brother if that was his favorite part of his trip to England, he answered no. I was perplexed and asked, "What was your favorite part of the trip then?"

My little brother proceeded to tell me about a very special "treasure hunt" he, his cousin, and his best friend (all age ten) had done, asking God for specific clues to find people He wanted them to meet and speak to on His behalf. Each one of these three boys made individual "treasure hunt lists" with information given to them by the Holy Spirit.

The adults didn't want to do it, but they took the kids out because they were so excited. As soon as they got out of the door, they spotted a family of seven sitting just across the street. They realized the three lists had details regarding the entire family, including what they were wearing and even their names! The kids shared the Gospel with the family, and the whole family got saved!

To really answer my question, my little brother concluded, "Luke, it was more important hearing God's voice and doing what He wanted me to do than to see someone coming out of a wheelchair because now those seven people are going to heaven, and they are going to spend their eternity with God. That's all."

Taken aback by the wisdom of my younger brother, I know that was a defining moment in my life because the way I viewed the things of God completely changed from that day onward. For the Lord "does not want anyone to perish, but everyone to come to repentance" (2 Peter 3:9b).

CANCER TAP

RICK LARSON / **CALIFORNIA, USA**

I was diagnosed with stage four esophageal cancer in 2008. My son wanted us to go to Bethel Healing Rooms, but at the time I wasn't a believer and didn't want to go. But as the diagnosis hit me and my fiancé, we decided to go.

As we entered the Healing Rooms, I had never seen a place with so much love, and I felt hope. I will never forget, I had my one son praying for me on one side, my younger son praying for me on the other side, and my fiancé praying behind me.

Suddenly a 12-year-old boy came bouncing towards me and said, "Rick Larson?" Immediately I was really mad and I thought to myself, *You've got to be kidding me! I drive 5 ½ hours, I'm sick with cancer and I've got a little boy to pray for me! I need Benny Hinn; I need pastor Bill Johnson; I need somebody anointed. Is everyone out for lunch?*

The next thing I knew, I felt this Presence coming over me and I remember thinking, "He's going to knock me over!" I had written on my Healing Rooms paperwork, "Do not touch me," but this boy, uninhibited, had come up and tapped me on the chest, and I went crashing down onto the ground under the power of God. After 45 minutes, I woke up on the carpet with a pillow under my head.

In disbelief, I was just lying there and the little boy was rubbing my chest. He said, "How are you feeling, Rick?"

Looking at the boy, I said, "Do you know what? My fear is gone!" The boy shouted, "Hallelujah!" There was a lady praying with this little boy and she asked me, "Rick, how do you feel inside?" As I became aware of my body, I said, "I feel like something has happened inside!" I replied in amazement. "I can feel warmth."

When I saw my family, I remember them saying, "Dad, you've got color!" I began to feel hungry and heavy. I knew then that it was done, that I was healed, and that God did something for me! I couldn't understand how or why He did it, but I know He did it.

I went back to the doctor and when he went to take x-rays of my esophagus, he said they were having trouble with the x-ray machine. I looked at the three images and there was a beam of light coming out of the center of each of the pictures. I called my son and told him about the pictures and he began to cry. He said to me, "Dad! Those are pictures of God. His Word says that He is the Light and He was in your throat, Dad! He was probably really busy. If He had known they were taking a picture He probably would have turned around and smiled!"

Today I serve in the Bethel Healing Rooms and there is no cancer anywhere in my body. Not only that, but God healed my blood pressure completely and I can still eat fast food!

74

KICKING OUT DEMONS

DANWA DE SILVA / **CALIFORNIA, USA**

When my boys were young, my husband and I were leading a Saturday night church service. During my husband's preaching, there was a lady who kept yelling, "I hate God!" At the end of the preaching we took time for prayer, and the intercessors were looking at me for direction on what to do for this lady. But I felt the Lord tell me to wait.

I went up to offer prayer, and the lady's friend came to me. I prayed with her and quick freedom came. She then grabbed her friend who had still been yelling, "I hate God!" She told her that she needed me to pray for her. She said, "I don't want her to pray!" but her friend convinced her to talk to me.

I sat down with her, and she began to tell me that she had come to church to make God angry because she was planning to go home and commit suicide and wanted to go to hell. I asked if she wanted to be free. We processed three mental pictures together, all having to do with friends of hers who had died unexpectedly. The Lord was showing her in each place where He was for them before they died, and that they were now with Him in heaven. The last picture she processed was of a friend of hers from high school. They had gone to the fair and went on a Ferris wheel together where he then died of an overdose.

Just then, my son Cory who was 12 at the time walked over and handed her a picture he'd drawn. He hadn't heard our conversation, but the picture was of her friend wearing the same shirt he'd worn on the Ferris wheel with his hands up to the Lord! She was amazed! I was then able to pray with her through deliverance, and it was extremely quick, only taking 3-5 minutes. Then I led her back to the Lord.

At the end, my eight year old son, Timmy, came over and said, "Mom, that was fun!" I said, "What was?" He said, "As soon as you sat down, I saw all the angels chasing off the demons. And it was weird, Mommy. At one point all the angels started dancing over her!" And I knew that heaven was rejoicing as she was saved.

NO SCHOOL NEEDED

MICHAEL MCMACKEN / **CALIFORNIA, USA**

I was suffering with a lot of pain from a carpal tunnel injury in my right wrist. I was told to have surgery, but my wife and I were moving to Redding to attend BSSM, so I said I would get healed when I got to Bethel.

My eight-year-old son William and I went to Redding from Washington State to look for a home for the rest of our family. While we were at Bethel Church, I had some individuals pray for me who I knew had success in praying for the sick, but I did not find healing from their prayers.

In the meantime, Bill Johnson asked those who were around people who wanted prayer to pray for them. My little boy William had never prayed for healing, but before I knew it, he said, "Papa, can I pray for you?" I said, "Of course, William." When he placed his hand on my wrist, he prayed, "Jesus, heal my Papa's wrist." In that moment, all my pain left and never returned!

William, knowing I was going to BSSM to learn to pray for healing, said, "Papa, I don't need to go to school. I know how to pray for healing."

TOUCH OF A BABY

CHUCK PARRY / **UNDISCLOSED**

I was leading a healing school at a large church in a rural farming community that had a good number of young families. As I was activating the congregation in healing, some of the young mothers mentioned to me that they used to be so much more involved in ministry and felt left out now that they spent so much time in the nursery. During the next ministry time, I asked that all the mothers bring their babies into the meeting, as they would be our ministry team. I had teams of mothers with babies laying hands on the sick and seeing great breakthrough.

One woman had bone cancer and had experienced so much pain and bone weakness that she often could not stand and had to use a wheelchair. Her pelvis and hips were riddled with cancer and the bones so fragile they feared any pressure or fall would fracture them.

The mothers circled around her and laid their babies' hands on the woman and declared "Life!" She felt a surge of energy and strength and got up and ran around the auditorium as the crowd cheered. Her situation was well known and there were many tears as she proclaimed that she was experiencing NO pain!

Another woman with MS told us in the next session that after prayer she had no pain and no longer experienced incontinence, which had been a major problem. The joy and freshness and the encouragement these mothers received were as exciting as the healing testimonies.

THROW OUT THE TRASH

BREANNA HILL / **OREGON, USA**

During the Compassion to Action Portland 2018 event, a young toddler came over to me during worship, picked a piece of paper off the ground, and handed it to me. I thanked him and put it on the seat next to me. A bit later he grabbed my hand and started pulling me to come with him.

I knew something was up, so I followed him down the stairs. He stopped me next to a woman in the front row of the stands, then he ran off giggling. I said to the woman, "Excuse me, ma'am, I think I'm supposed to pray for you." She told me she had knee pain that had been prayed for three times without improvement. I prayed for her knees and had her stand up to test them out, but her right knee was no better.

Just then the little boy came back and grabbed my hand to pull me away. I told the woman I'd come back to pray with her more. The toddler ran ahead and came back with a crumpled McDonald's bag filled with trash, which he handed to me. He then ran to the foot of the stairs, giggling, pointed up to where I'd been sitting, then sprinted around in a circle.

Immediately, I knew what Holy Spirit was doing. I retrieved the piece of paper the boy had handed me earlier, crumpled it up, and took it to the woman. I asked her if there was something recently going on in her life that she wanted to throw away. She looked shocked and started crying.

She shared that she had two close family members who were living in sin. She was worried for their salvation, and her heart was breaking because she loved them so much. I shared a prophetic picture of Jesus holding her and her two family members in his hands, and I asked her if she could see it. She said yes, so I asked her where Jesus was in the picture and what he was saying. She said, "He says, 'They're mine,'" and she wept for a while as I sang over her.

When she was done, I had her throw the piece of paper into the McDonald's bag as a prophetic act of letting go. Then I said a quick prayer for her knees, and they were completely healed!

It was so beautiful to partner with the Holy Spirit and a toddler in ministry!

T-I-M

PAM OEHLBERG / **NEW JERSEY, USA**

At our church in New Jersey, we teach our kids from an early age how to hear the voice of the Lord and to come to services ready to minister. We have a 12-year-old named Arsen in our children's church with an emotional disability that prevents him from expressing what he needs. When faced with challenges, he acts out his frustration like a much younger child.

However, one day Arsen was asked to wait on the Lord and listen for an encouraging word for someone in class. He quieted down and set his heart to listen. As he waited, Arsen suddenly saw a picture of the Father writing the letters T-I-M on the palm of His hand. He asked the teacher if she knew someone named Tim, and her eyes filled with tears. It was her son's name. He had fallen away from the Lord ans was struggling with an addiction and it was a heavy burden on her heart.

Arsen went on to share that "the Lord says He has Tim in the palm of His hand." God pinpointed her burden and assured her He was moving in his life!

Our children's pastor has also taught the children how to hear the voice of the Lord to write their own psalms. Arsen wrote this beautiful song of worship:

Forever, the Greatest ever! Majestic!
God You will last forever!
Your greatness will continue for ALWAYS!
You are Great God!
Now and forever.
Anyone who KNOWS you,
KNOWS how majestic You are, My God!

Love, Arsen

DANCING ENCOUNTERS

KIANA MATTSON / **CALIFORNIA, USA**

My name is Kiana, I'm nine years old and I love to dance!

One day I was dancing with my little sister in the Healing Rooms ministry in our church. I saw a team leader praying for a man. We found out later he had back pain, but she wasn't seeing any progress for his healing. When she saw us dancing, God told her to have us come and dance over him.

So my sister and I went and danced around the man. Almost immediately he went right into an encounter with God and fell flat on the floor. It was surprising to him because he'd never had an encounter with God before. God's presence was so strong that the team leader said she could hardly stand.

It made me feel really happy and thankful that God could use my little sister and me as we did what we loved to do!

WHO CARRIES AN EPIPEN?

ZACHARY SMITHEE / **COLORADO, USA**

I had a life-threatening sesame allergy and carried an EpiPen.

One Sunday at Bridgeway Church in Denver, Colorado, the children shared a word of knowledge that God wanted to heal someone with an EpiPen. I responded and went to receive prayer from the children. The children prayed for God to fill me with His Spirit and for my allergy to be healed. To be honest, I was doubtful I would be healed because the last time I had eaten sesame in hummus, I had gone into anaphylactic shock and my throat closed, requiring medication to help me.

Two days later I was with a group of friends standing around the kitchen at a friend's house after a worship night. The mother of the house had made some Asian food. We were hungry, and so without thinking too much, we dug in. After nearly finishing, we jokingly asked whether there was any sesame in the dish. We were alarmed to find out that the beef had been cooked in sesame oil!

My symptoms—vomiting and then a closed throat—usually kick in within 30 minutes. I didn't have my EpiPen with me. I waited and waited, but for the first time, I wasn't experiencing any of these symptoms. I knew there was an ER around the corner; however, after an hour, I still had no symptoms. Our friends celebrated, thanked God and rejoiced. I was healed!

Who carries an Epipen?

06

PETS

HEALING DOGS & SAVING OWNERS

GINNY GRIMES / CALIFORNIA, USA

Two years ago, when he was eight years old, our son Justus was out on a treasure hunt, asking God to give him specific clues for someone who needed prayer. After writing down the clues, we ventured out and he suddenly spotted a woman that matched almost every clue on his list.

When he started talking to her, she was not open to receiving prayer. But Justus and the team could tell that her dog's back hips were really messed up. The dog had a collar with a heart tag and Justus had a heart necklace on his list of things to look for. When he asked the lady if he could pray for her dog, she replied that her dog had metal in each hip and she would love prayer for him.

The team prayed for the dog, whose back legs were very rigid with hardly any mobility. After they prayed, the dog was leaping and jumping like a puppy! It is pretty safe to say that all of the metal in the dog's hips had dissolved. The lady was so shocked that she then asked the team to pray for her back, which was injured years prior. The team prayed, and the lady was instantly healed of her back pain. Justus then asked the lady if she wanted to receive Jesus as her Lord and Savior. She said yes, and Justus led the lady to the Lord!

YOU WILL LIVE AND NOT DIE

GINNY GRIMES / CALIFORNIA, USA

Our family dog, Molly, was throwing up and had horrible diarrhea. When we took her to the vet, they said she had swallowed something, and they would need to do surgery to remove whatever was blocking her intestines. The surgery would cost a few thousand dollars, and we didn't have the money.

We were praying that the blockage would come out on its own, but days went by, and Molly was not improving. I was feeding her with a syringe, but there was still no progress. One night before bed, I told our four children to say goodbye to Molly because she wasn't going to live through the night. Three of them crowded around her and instantly started crying. Justus, our four-year-old little boy, came over and said, "Hey guys, why are you crying? We should be praying!"

He then started speaking in tongues. One of our girls started singing the most beautiful song in the Spirit. And our other two girls started to intensely declare, "Molly, you will live and not die. Molly, we speak life into your body. Molly, Jesus is making you new!" This went on for minutes as my husband and I stood in awe at the faith of our children.

I asked Jesus what I should do, and I felt like I was supposed to call Molly to the back door, knowing she hadn't moved for days. I said, "Molly, come!" and up she jumped! She ran straight out the door, did two laps around our backyard, and then squatted and pooped out the stinkiest big old rock! She came inside, ate and drank, and she is still living today!

KIDS

FAITH FOR A CAT

ARIEL ANNA LYNCH / CALIFORNIA, USA

My name is Ariel, and I'm 14 years old. During our summer vacation we found out that our cat Sunshine had left our house. We thought he would come back after a few days, but he didn't. After three months, he was still not there, so we prayed. We prayed for one month, then two, then three. By this time we had lost hope. We decided that he had found a new home or had peacefully died somewhere.

Then five months had passed since Sunshine went missing, and we had gotten used to the fact that he was gone. We thought he'd come back when it got cold, but he didn't. When we went to church one Sunday, our pastor was talking about how we should not let our faith die. He also talked a little about what a prayer of faith is. He said that a prayer of faith isn't when you pray once with extraordinary faith and it happens, but it's when you keep praying no matter if it happened yet or not. This reminded me that I had given up on my prayer for Sunshine, so I decided that week I'd pray.

That Thursday I remembered and I took a moment to pray during school. It was a quick, easy prayer. I simply said, "God, please bring Sunshine back." That evening we were getting out of the car, and there he was! He walked up to us out of nowhere, and the weird thing is that he was bigger, fatter, and healthier. This happened so fast! And it's amazing to think God took the time to make sure our furry friend came back.

HAMSTER RESURRECTION

DAVE HARVEY / CALIFORNIA, USA

The boys and I had decided to take a risk and let the hamster go for a scurry around the kitchen and experience freedom from its cage. The thing which made this extra dangerous was that this cute little furball had been loaned to us for a few weeks, from a family that went on a trip back to their home country.

I was watching the boys nervously and said, "Hey, let's be careful he doesn't go...," and before I could get the words out, the hamster ran underneath our trash can. "Oh no!" we exclaimed as we ran to make sure we didn't lose it underneath the refrigerator. My eldest son Zeke looked and looked for it and then decided to stand on the foot lever that opened up the bin. Again, before I could finish the sentence "Be careful when you push the pedal you don't...," the little hamster poked his head out right where the pedal pushed down, and without seeing him, Zeke accidentally released the foot lever and the furry little fluff ball became more of a pancake! "Oh no! He's squashed!" We all shrieked as we looked at the lifeless, suspended rodent, stuck in the air between the foot pedal and the base of the bin.

We carefully engaged the foot pedal and pulled him out. He was flatter, had stopped breathing and his tongue was sticking out of his mouth like a cartoon. Instantly, I said, "Guys, quick! Let's pray for a resurrection!" So the boys gathered around, and as I held the little guy in my hand, they began to pray for him. We prayed and nothing happened, so we prayed again. We kept praying for about one minute, and the hamster didn't move. Then we prayed one more time, and suddenly his little chest inhaled air. He was alive! We thanked Jesus for saving the hamster and, rather relieved, quickly placed him back into his cage!

THREE VETS AND NO TUMOR

SARA SYNN / CALIFORNIA, USA

I took our three-year-old dog, Todd, to the vet for an annual check up, and we received terrible news that he had an alarming tumor in his neck that could be cancerous. We were going to have to monitor him closely and take him for a biopsy in a couple of weeks.

When I broke the news to my brothers, eleven-year-old Paul and nine-year-old Michael, the first thing out of Paul's mouth was that he wanted to pray for God to heal him. We prayed right then and there. Michael suggested we pray every day until the next appointment where they would take a biopsy.

When we took Todd for the biopsy, they were shocked because the tumor had completely disappeared! They had three different vets check because they were so confused about where it went. I told my brothers with tears in my eyes, and we all screamed with joy. I explained to them that God cares about the things that concern us and that He hears every prayer. Today Todd is a completely healthy dog, and my brothers love to pray for healing for both humans and animals!

BUNNY BRAINS

SCOTT BILEUI / CALIFORNIA, USA

O ur teenage kids recently had a fun experience. They have rabbits just like I did when I grew up and recently their rabbits had a litter of bunnies. Sadly, one of them was born with a birth defect. We don't know how it was alive, because it was missing half its skull. It was really weird to look at.

My kids know about and have constantly celebrated my bunny testimony from over twenty years ago. It was an amazing story of how God answered my prayer as a seven-year-old and gave my blind bunny eyeballs overnight (see page 6).

So after the kids put the bunny away that night, my daughter went into her room and prayed that God would do it again. The next morning the bunny's skull was perfectly whole!

07

TRY THIS AT HOME!

HOLY SPIRIT BIRTHDAYS

ANDREW PHILLIPS / PROPHECY

On birthday meals as a family, we've made it a tradition to prophesy over the person having a birthday. At first, I had to talk them through it. It'd go something like, "All right. We're going to hear God's voice about Noah" (or whoever the birthday person was). Then I'd say, "All right, connect with Holy Spirit, and you'll feel something," and they all knew that as they leaned back into the arms of the Holy Spirit, they'd feel love, joy or peace just as the Bible says (Galatians 5:22). Usually when I'd ask them what they were feeling, peace was the first thing. One would feel Him on their shoulders, while another would feel Him on their chest. (It was great as a parent to hear them one after another say how they could feel peace on different parts of their bodies.)

Then I'd say, "Put your hands on your head when you have connected with Holy Spirit and feel love, peace or joy." After the kids would do it, I'd say, "All right, now ask Holy Spirit for an animal, or a tree, or a movie or something. Put your hands on your head once you've got that." And they'd do that.

Finally when everyone had hands on their heads, I'd say, "Right, what is it about that animal or movie that's kind or encouraging that God wants to say to the person? Once you've got an encouraging word, hands on your head. Remember to ask yourself, 'Does this word coincide with God's character? Does it sound like God?' If the answer is yes, wrap it up and deliver it as a message."

We'd then go around the table, and the children would deliver their prophetic words for the person we were celebrating. This has worked fantastically, and now the kids just do it automatically. I'll start to say, "All right, put your hands on your head," and the kids will exclaim, "Yeah, yeah, we're already there, Dad." I'll say, "Right, ask Holy Spirit..." and they'll remark, "Dad, I've already chosen a movie!" It's so much fun to see how easily the kids can connect with Holy Spirit, hear His voice and build others up!

STICKY NOTE PRAYERS

RITA, REVIVAL MINISTRIES / **PRAYER**

I moved to Redding ten years ago with my four kids, and we had nothing but backpacks. By the grace of God, we found a rental and slowly began to rebuild our lives. The kids had been through loss and abuse. The situation created a real need within us to pray.

Unbeknownst to me, my eight-year-old son was praying for signs that God existed. One afternoon he came running up to me yelling, "God's not answering my prayers!"

Being a single mom with four small kids meant I was always answering a considerable number of questions. I had explanations and teachings for every question. However, when my son asked me why God would not answer, it was not a teaching moment. It was important that my son see God show up.

I called my kids together, and, handing them two sticky notes each, I instructed them to write down a prayer on each one and put the notes on the door in the hallway.

The prayers ranged from small to large. I commissioned my children to pray the prayers on the notes every time they walked by the door. When a prayer had been answered, I'd pull the note off the door, leaving a blank spot to indicate God's answered prayer.

Over the months, the notes came off the door one by one, restoring faith, until there was only one left. The last note read, "a car for mommy." This note was written by my eight-year-old son. That note remained for quite a while and lost its stickiness. We put tape on and continued re-taping. We were relentless in our prayers to have that note come down.

One day I was at the table when a set of keys landed in front of me. A friend of mine had come over as a surprise to give me a paid-off car! They had no idea we were praying for one. My son came home from school, I walked him down the hall, and asked him to take off the last note. He cried. He wasn't crying over a car; he was crying in restored faith. God showed up.

Children's prayers are fierce. But so is their doubt at times. Sometimes we need to set teaching aside and ask God for action.

— Rita

God is not bound to act according to what we believe about Him. Rather, we are bound to believe Him as He demonstrates Himself to us.

—Beni Johnson

ASK, PRAY, TEST

SUE CARPENTER / HEALING

I was one of the kids' leaders for Awakening Australia. When I was teaching the kids about healing, I shared about a dream I had. I was walking in a garden, and I heard a child's voice saying, "Do you want to play?" I felt my heart leap as I said yes.

I turned to see who had said it, and it was a young boy. I realized this boy was Jesus! He laughed, and we began to play in the garden. We took two wide blades of grass and made them hum with our lips. We found sycamore seeds and threw them up to watch them spin like helicopters. We pinched dragon flower heads open and fastened them on our shirts. We were laughing and having so much fun.

After a while He looked up, excited, and asked again, "Do you want to play?" With joy I said yes. He clapped His hands and said, "Let's play heal the sick, raise the dead, set the captives free!" Then I woke up.

I shared with the kids how much fun it was to play with Jesus and we taught them how to heal the sick with Him. We told them first to "ask" if you can pray for the person, second to "pray" in Jesus' name, and third, to "test" and have them check if there's been a change. We taught them to celebrate any change, and if they weren't 100% better yet, to pray again!

We then released the children to "play with Jesus" in their groups. Afterwards, two six-year-old girls ran up to tell me their story. When they were in their group time, one girl had a bad headache. She was crying from the pain, so her friend said, "Let's do the 'ask, pray, test.'"

So she asked, "Can we pray for you?" and the kids in the group prayed. Then she asked what happened. The girl replied, "It was like Jesus came and put a band-aid on my forehead!" All the pain was gone. Just then the mom arrived to bring the girl some Panadol. All the kids yelled out, "She doesn't need it. Jesus healed her!"

TRY THIS AT HOME!

VIDEO TUTORIALS

Check out **increasekidsbook.com** for video activation teaching kids how to step into the supernatural life with Jesus:

Hear God's Voice

Prophecy God's Love

Heal the Sick

...And More!

WWW.INCREASEKIDSBOOK.COM

"I WANT LITTLE CHILDREN TO COME TO ME, SO NEVER INTERFERE WITH THEM WHEN THEY WANT TO COME..."

MATTHEW 19:14, TPT

I always knew I wanted to work with children, and in college I decided to major in Christian Education. Though I grew up in the church, in my first year of college I came to know the Holy Spirit in a whole new way. The pastor of the local church I was attending had just come back from the Toronto Blessing, and one night at church I saw and experienced things I never knew were possible. It was exciting, but I mostly felt afraid because I had no idea what was happening. This caused me to run into the Father's arms and ask a whole lot of questions.

At one point my family told me my experience was of the Devil and to get away from it as quickly as possible. I found that I had to put all my trust in God as I journeyed to discover the Holy Spirit in a new way. My discovery of Him came through His Word, His fruit, and what God was saying to me. When I became a mother I realized I had to help steward and foster this relationship for the next generation and the generations to follow.

For the past two decades I have watched the Children's Department at Bethel Church experience the most amazing miracles that are coming from the mouths, hands, and hearts of the children. Children have a faith that is strong, steady, and simple. They read and hear who God is, and they believe He is who He says He is and will do what He said He can do. Because they have so much less to mentally overcome than adults, they are able to see spiritual things that would normally paralyze the mind and heart of a believing adult. They know who they are, they know who they carry, and they know what authority they have.

Can you imagine your home, your church, your city, and your country with children walking so freely in this identity married with faith? What could that level of faith do? We must look at our children as an investment and start as early as we can to bring our children into a real and tangible relationship with God the Father, Christ Jesus, and the Holy Spirit. They must know they have been created for a mandate and purpose that is far beyond our wildest dreams.

They were given to us as one of the best gifts and we have one of the greatest responsibilities to deposit all we can into them. They are the next generation. If our ceiling is going to be their floor, we must give them everything we have at any cost. Our hope is they will take our investment in them and experience exponential growth with their faith married with God's promises. "For nothing is impossible with God" (Luke 1:37).

AMY GAGNON

CHILDREN'S PASTOR, BETHEL CHRISTIAN SCHOOL

Celebrate His Goodness.

Increase Testimony app is about celebrating the goodness of God through the power of testimony.

Share your testimony and watch God do it again!

Increase Testimony is available on the App Store and Google Play.

TELL YOUR STORY

---

*IF THIS BOOK HAS IMPACTED YOUR LIFE,
PLEASE TAKE A FEW MINUTES TO SEND US AN
EMAIL AND TELL US YOUR STORY.*

MYSTORY@INCREASE.GLOBAL

LEARN MORE:

🌐 *WWW.INCREASE.GLOBAL*

📷 *@INCREASE.GLOBAL*

ⓕ *FACEBOOK.COM/INCREASE.GLOBAL*